Soups, Salads & Snacks

NATURALLY FAST RECIPES

LEON

Soups, Salads & Snacks

NATURALLY FAST RECIPES

By Henry Dimbleby, Kay Plunkett-Hogge, Claire Ptak & John Vincent

PHOTOGRAPHY BY GEORGIA GLYNN SMITH · DESIGN BY ANITA MANGAN

conran
OCTOPUS

Contents

Introduction

Leon was founded on the belief that food should taste good and do you good. We wanted to make it easy for everyone to eat this way.

The recipes in this book are designed to help you do just that. They are created from a small number of easy-to-find ingredients, and the vast majority have five steps or fewer. It is food you can make quickly from scratch. None of the recipes take more than 20 minutes to prepare—with the exception of Benny's Scotch Eggs (see page 44) and Ana's Cheese Empanadas (see page 46), which reward the time investment handsomely. You can let your oven do the rest and kick back with a glass of wine or some other libation, depending on your preference.

It is also a little book. We want it to become a companion, one that you take with you on vacation, or away for the weekend,or, painful though it is to consider, to give to that beloved child on the day they fly the nest.

While quick, the recipes (selected from the best in the full-sized Leon cookbooks) have been chosen for their variety. The soups range from the scented and exotic: Apple's Persian Onion Soup (see page 10), to the homespun and comforting: Bacon & Root Veg Soup (see page 23).

In the salad chapter you will find things that are absurdly quick and perfect for supper; try Bean Salad with Pickled Onions (see page 26) or Mackerel Skies Salad (see page 39). For something more glamorous that could form the centerpiece of a summer lunch try Laura's Jeweled Salad (see page 28).

In the snacks chapter we hope to provide a little inspiration for those snack attacks and munchies moments. You will find imaginative toppings for baked potatoes (see page 48) and for toast (see page 54). There are quick dips (see page 56) and the Leon bestselling Fish Stick Wrap (see page 52).

Whichever recipes really grab you, we hope you use this book again and again, and that in 20 years' time it is still in your kitchen—dog-eared and sauce-splattered, but loved. Happy cooking!

Henry & John

Apple's Persian Onion Soup

A favorite recipe from the restaurants—very healthy, and great if you are feeling under par.

4 large **onions**
2 tablespoons **olive oil**
1 heaping teaspoon **turmeric**
1 heaping teaspoon **ground fenugreek**
1 teaspoon **dried mint**
4 cups **chicken** or **vegetable stock**
1 **cinnamon stick**
½ a **lemon**
sea salt and **freshly ground black pepper**

1. Peel the onions and slice them thinly. Put the onions into a large saucepan with the olive oil over low heat. Add some salt and pepper, cover, and cook for at least 15 minutes, stirring occasionally.

2. Add the turmeric, fenugreek, and mint, and cook, uncovered, for another few minutes.

3. Add the stock and cinnamon stick, bring to a boil, then reduce the heat and simmer for at least 20 minutes.

4. Add the juice of half a lemon. Season with salt and pepper and serve. We like to leave the cinnamon stick in.

My best friend Sophie Douglas Bate is the most incredible chef from Edible Food Design, and we have cooked and traveled together for years. Her family used to live in Tehran and this became a staple soup in our lives—great for when you are trying to lose weight.

APPLE

TIPS

* Add some chopped fresh mint and parsley at the end to liven things up.

* Apple adds a teaspoon of sugar for added sweetness—we leave this out.

Kay's Minestrone Maltese

When Kay's parents first moved to Gozo, in Malta, they made friends with some of the local farmers who had fields on the slopes below their house. One of those farmers taught them the basis of this soup. This is not a thin soup; it's hearty, filling, and packed with flavor.

1–2 tablespoons **olive oil**
1 **onion**, 1 **carrot**, and 1 stick of **celery**, diced
2 cloves of **garlic**, minced
1 teaspoon **fresh rosemary**, chopped
5 cups **vegetable stock**
1 x 15-oz can of **diced tomatoes**
1 **bay leaf**
1 piece of **Parmesan rind** (optional)
1 x 15-oz can of **cannellini beans**, drained and rinsed

3 oz little **pasta shapes**
1 cup **peas**
1 **zucchini**, trimmed and cubed
a good grating of **nutmeg**
2½ oz **bacon**, diced and cooked (optional)
a few **celery leaves**, chopped
freshly grated **Parmesan cheese**, to garnish
salt and **freshly ground black pepper**

1. Heat the oil in a large, heavy saucepan over low to medium heat. Add the onion, carrot, celery, and garlic and soften gently for about 5 minutes. Then add the rosemary and cook for another 2 minutes or so to release its oils.

2. Now add the stock, tomatoes, bay leaf, and the Parmesan rind (if you're using it), and cook for about 5 minutes. Season with salt and pepper, add the beans, and simmer for another 15 minutes or so.

3. Add the pasta, and cook according to the package instructions until done. About 5 minutes before the end, add the remaining vegetables and diced bacon.

4. Finally, add a couple of gratings of fresh nutmeg and stir it into the soup. Then season to taste and add the bacon (if you are using it).

5. Serve garnished with chopped celery leaves and a grating of Parmesan.

TIPS

* Minestrone simply means "a big soup," so you can pretty much put anything you like into it. Instead of the peas, why not add about ¾ lb of trimmed and sliced kale or chard?

* If I want to add some bacon, I tend to cook it in a separate pan and offer it as an optional garnish, which means I can serve this as a completely vegetarian soup.

Marion's Lentil Soup

If chicken noodle soup is Jewish penicillin, this is North London Protestant penicillin. Marion, John's mom, makes this for the family when it's cold outside, or when people have colds. Make plenty in advance, and get it out of the freezer whenever the feeling or the need arises.

1 tablespoon **olive oil**
1 large **onion**, diced
2 **leeks**, sliced
1 clove of **garlic**, crushed
4 slices of **smoked bacon**, chopped
2 **carrots**, sliced
3 sticks of **celery**, sliced
1 cup **red lentils**, washed and drained
½ teaspoon **grated nutmeg** or **turmeric**
5 cups **vegetable** or **chicken stock**
salt and **freshly ground black pepper**

1. Heat the oil in a large heavy saucepan over low heat. Add the onions and leeks and let them cook gently until they're transparent. Add the garlic and bacon and cook on medium heat for another 3–4 minutes.

2. Now stir in the carrots and celery, and cook for a further 2–3 minutes. Finally, stir in the lentils, and add the nutmeg or turmeric.

3. Pour in the stock and bring the soup to a boil. Simmer with the lid on for about 30–40 minutes, or until the lentils and vegetables are tender. Season the soup with salt and pepper, then blend until smooth.

TIPS

* Marion prefers to use an immersion blender for this recipe. If you're using a stand blender be very careful not to overfill it so you don't spatter the kitchen (and yourself) with boiling soup.

* For a thicker consistency use more carrots and/or celery.

Leek & Potato Soup

SERVES 4 • PREPARATION TIME: 20 MINUTES • COOKING TIME: 45 MINUTES • WF GF V

This is the simplest and most soothing soup I know, and perfect for a stormy winter's day.

¾ lb **leeks**, cleaned and sliced
3–4 Yukon Gold **potatoes**, peeled and cut into chunks
2 teaspoons **sea salt**
4 cups **water**
½ cup **heavy cream**
1 tablespoon chopped **fresh flat-leaf parsley**
freshly ground black pepper

1. Put the leeks and potatoes into a heavy saucepan over medium heat. Add the salt and the water and bring to a boil. Reduce the heat and simmer for about 30–35 minutes, or until the vegetables are soft and cooked through. Then turn off the heat and, with an immersion blender, blend until smooth.

2. Stir the cream into the soup, then add the parsley and a few grindings of black pepper. Taste and adjust the seasoning. Serve with crusty bread.

Roasted Pumpkin Soup with a Zing

Creamy and comforting, this brightly colored soup will cheer up even the darkest fall day. To jazz it up a bit, we've added ground cumin and coriander for warmth.

4 lbs **pumpkin**, seeded, cut in wedges
3–4 sprigs of **fresh thyme**
2 tablespoons **olive oil**
3 cups good-quality **vegetable** or **chicken stock**
1–2 teaspoons **ground cumin**
1–2 teaspoons **ground coriander**
2 **limes**, cut into wedges, to serve
2 teaspoons **dried red pepper flakes**,
   to garnish
salt and **freshly ground black pepper**

1. Heat the oven to 350°F.

2. Put the pumpkin wedges and the thyme into a large roasting pan, coat with the olive oil, and season with salt and pepper. Place in the oven for 45 minutes to an hour, or until it's really soft and tender. Note, it could take even longer—every pumpkin is different—just keep checking on it until it's done.

3. When the pumpkin is cooked, set it aside to cool, then scrape the flesh away from the skin. If it comes away in whole slices, cut it into ¾-inch chunks. Then put it into a pan with the stock and blend with an immersion blender until you have a creamy consistency.

4. Add the spices and heat through for about 5 minutes. Then taste and add seasoning.

5. Serve in bowls, with the lime wedges and little piles of dried red pepper flakes on the side.

Belinda's Chicken Noodle Soup

SERVES 4 • PREPARATION TIME: 10 MINUTES • COOKING TIME: 10 MINUTES • ♥ ✓WF GF DF

A quick and healthy weeknight supper.

    4 cups **chicken stock**
    2 **chicken breasts**
    2 cloves of **garlic**
    8 oz mixed **shiitake** and **chestnut mushrooms**
    4 oz **bok choy**
    a large handful of **fresh cilantro**
    2 tablespoons **peanut oil**
    8 oz **rice noodles**
    3 tablespoons **soy sauce**
    2 tablespoons **toasted sesame oil**

1. Put the chicken stock into a large saucepan, cover, and bring to a boil. Meanwhile, cut the chicken breasts into small chunks.

2. Peel and finely slice the garlic. Generously slice the mushrooms. Chop the bok choy and cilantro roughly.

3. Pour the peanut oil into a hot wok or wide heavy saucepan over high heat. When it smokes, add the garlic just for a few seconds and immediately follow with the chicken and mushrooms. Keep tossing until cooked (about 5–7 minutes). Add the soy sauce and sesame oil and keep tossing until absorbed.

4. Add the rice noodles and bok choy to the hot chicken stock, cover, and boil for 3–4 minutes. Pour the contents of the wok into the pan of stock and noodles and sprinkle with the cilantro. Eat immediately.

Belinda, my stepmother, appears effortlessly to combine managing a large extended family, a doctorate, and a new career in psychology with the production of enormous feasts whenever family and friends descend on her house (which is quite often). This is one of her staple meals.

HENRY

TIPS

* Depending on what brand of rice noodles you use, you may need to add extra stock—some soak up more liquid than others.

* A squeeze of lime on top before you eat is a nice addition.

Bacon & Root Veg Soup

SERVES 4–6 • PREPARATION TIME: 20 MINUTES • COOKING TIME: 30 MINUTES • ✓ WF GF

A winter warmer and a Mima staple.

4 oz **bacon**
1 large **onion**
2 large **carrots**
½ **rutabaga**
3 Yukon Gold or white round **potatoes**
3 **parsnips**
2 tablespoons **olive oil**
2 **bay leaves**
6½ cups **chicken stock**
1 cup shredded **Cheddar** or **Parmesan cheese**
sea salt and **freshly ground black pepper**

1. Cut the bacon into small pieces. Peel and chop the onion. Peel and cube the carrots, rutabaga, potatoes, and parsnips.

2. Heat the oil in a heavy saucepan. Add the bacon and fry until it is just getting crispy. Add the onion, and cook until it is getting soft.

3. Add all the cubed vegetables and the bay leaves, cover with a lid, and cook over low heat for 10 minutes, stirring occasionally.

4. Add the stock and simmer for 15 minutes, or until the vegetables are tender.

5. Remove and discard the bay leaves. Season to taste and serve in bowls, sprinkled with the cheese.

TIPS

* Vegetarians can use garlic instead of the bacon, and vegetable stock instead of chicken stock.

* You can use any surplus root vegetables you have lying around. Celeriac tastes great alongside, or instead of, the parsnips.

Bean Salad with Pickled Onions

SERVES 4 • PREPARATION TIME: 15 MINUTES • COOKING TIME: NONE • ♥ ✓ WF GF DF V

Simple, fresh, and healthy—pickling the onions like this sweetens them and takes away the raw onion flavor.

1 clove of **garlic**
1 **lemon**
a large handful of chopped
   fresh flat-leaf parsley
1 large **red onion**
2 medium **vine-ripened tomatoes**
2 tablespoons **extra virgin olive oil**
2 x 15-oz cans of **cannellini beans**, drained and rinsed
sea salt and **freshly ground black pepper**

1. Peel the garlic. On the finest holes of your grater, grate the garlic and lemon zest and mix it in a small bowl with the chopped parsley.

2. Peel the red onion and slice it as finely as you can. Put the slices into a large salad bowl with a few pinches of sea salt and the lemon juice. Let stand for 5 minutes.

3. Chop the tomatoes into coarse chunks and add them to the onions. Season with salt then add the olive oil and the beans. Toss really well to combine the flavors. Season.

4. Let the salad sit until you get a nice pooling of tomato juice at the bottom—the magic juice. This will take around 5–10 minutes.

5. Stir in the parsley, lemon, and garlic mixture, and serve.

TIPS

* Serve with sourdough toast for a simple supper.

* Add toasted seeds or almonds.

* Substitute other fresh green herbs for the parsley.

* There are three things that raise this dish above the ordinary: the pickled onions; letting it sit so the juices steep; and the raw parsley, lemon, and garlic mixture added at the end. You can try all kinds of combinations of different beans and vegetables (raw, grated zucchini are a great addition, as are grated carrots).

Laura's Jeweled Salad

1 cup **barley coucous**
8 oz good-quality **feta cheese**
1 **cucumber**
a bunch of mixed **fresh green herbs**,
   e.g. **mint** and **cilantro**
¾ cup **pine nuts**
seeds of 1 large **pomegranate**
2 cloves of **garlic**
2 tablespoons **extra virgin olive oil**
juice of 1½ **lemons**
sea salt and **freshly ground black pepper**

1. Prepare the couscous following the package instructions. Let cool in a large bowl.

2. Crumble the feta and slice the cucumber into chunks. Add these to the bowl, then roughly tear the herbs and add them, too.

3. Lightly toast the pine nuts in a skillet over low heat. When they turn a light golden color, scatter them, along with the pomegranate seeds, onto the salad.

4. Peel and finely mince or grate the garlic. Whisk together the olive oil, lemon juice, and garlic and pour the dressing onto the salad. Toss gently to coat, season well with salt and pepper, and serve.

Thirtieth Birthday Pea Salad

SERVES 4 • PREPARATION TIME: 5 MINUTES • COOKING TIME: 10 MINUTES • ♥ ✓ WF GF DF V

1 **red** bell **pepper**
1-inch piece of **fresh ginger**
2 cloves of **garlic**
6 **scallions**
2 tablespoons **extra virgin olive oil**
1 teaspoon **black mustard seeds**
1 teaspoon **red wine vinegar**
1⅔ cups **frozen peas**
a small handful of **fresh cilantro**, washed
 and chopped
sea salt and **freshly ground black pepper**

1. Halve and seed the pepper, and cut into slices. Peel and grate the ginger and garlic. Trim the scallions and cut on the diagonal into long thin strips.

2. Heat the olive oil in a saucepan over medium heat. Add the mustard seeds and fry until they pop. Swirl in the garlic and ginger.

3. Add the pepper, stirring well until it picks up some color. Add the scallions and the vinegar. It will sizzle a bit.

4. Throw in the peas with a tiny splash of water and let defrost and then warm up, stirring occasionally. You are not aiming to cook them, just to get them up to room temperature.

5. Remove from the heat. Season and add the chopped cilantro to serve.

I first made this salad at my joint 30th birthday party with my friends Simon and Roly. We made it for about 150 people, dressing it by tossing it in (clean) black garbage bags—a useful trick.

HENRY

Carrots & Beets WITH SLIVERED ALMONDS

SERVES 4 • PREPARATION TIME: 5 MINUTES • COOKING TIME: 45 MINUTES • ♥ ✓ WF GF DF V

Beautiful to look at and extremely straightforward to make.

9 whole **raw beets** (about 1¾ lbs), peeled and cut into chunks
10 **carrots** (about 1¾ lbs), peeled and quartered lengthwise
¼ cup **extra virgin olive oil**
1½ tablespoons **honey**
1 tablespoon **balsamic vinegar**
¾ cup **slivered almonds**
3 tablespoons chopped **fresh chervil** or **parsley leaves** (optional)
sea salt and **freshly ground black pepper**

1. Preheat the oven to 400°F.

2. Put the beets and carrots into separate oven dishes, coat with olive oil, and season well with salt and pepper. Add the honey to the carrots and the balsamic vinegar to the beets and stir well.

3. Put both dishes into the oven for 45 minutes, or until the carrots are starting to brown and the beets are soft.

4. Meanwhile, toast the almonds in a dry skillet over medium heat on the stove, being careful not to burn them.

5. Place the vegetables on a serving dish. Scatter with the chervil or parsley, if using, and the almonds, and serve.

Warm Anchovy, Garlic & Potato Salad

SERVES 4 • PREPARATION TIME: 5 MINUTES • COOKING TIME: 20 MINUTES • ♥ WF GF DF

Pouring a dressing onto warm potatoes has a wonderful effect, because the potatoes soften and absorb the flavors. This dish is very addictive.

1¾ lbs **new potatoes**
3 cloves of **garlic**
2 tablespoons **white wine vinegar**
1 x 2-oz **can of anchovy fillets**
½ cup **extra virgin olive oil**
1 tablespoon finely chopped **fresh chives**
sea salt and **freshly ground black pepper**

1. Chop the potatoes in half and cook them, covered, in a large pan of boiling salted water until tender.

2. Put the garlic, vinegar, and anchovies into a blender and blend to form a paste. With the blender running, drizzle in the extra virgin olive oil. Season.

3. Drain the potatoes and pour the dressing over them, tossing them well.

4. Let cool for 3 minutes, then toss again. Sprinkle with the chopped chives and serve.

TIPS

* It is a good idea to cut the potatoes in half with a fork once cooked, so that they are roughed up and absorb the anchovy dressing.

* You can use parsley in the place of chives.

* If you can't get hold of new potatoes, any white round or red-skinned potatoes will do. If you use bigger ones, peel them and chop them into chunks.

* Great as a side salad at a barbecue. Make it in the morning and serve it later at room temperature.

3 Sisters Superfood Salad

SERVES 4 • PREPARATION TIME: 15–20 MINUTES • COOKING TIME: 35 MINUTES • ♥ ✓ DF V

These 3 sisters—corn, beans, and squash—and their friends really pack a punch: a vibrant, delicious, colorful salad that showcases big, bold flavors influenced by the fusion of the new and old worlds.

¾ lb **pumpkin**, peeled, seeded, and cut into 1–1½-inch cubes (about 3 cups)

4–6 small **purple potatoes**

a little **olive oil**

2 **cobs of corn**

4 large handfuls of **mixed greens**

2 cups **bean** and **seed sprouts**

4 **scallions**, trimmed and sliced on the diagonal

1 **avocado**, cut into ¾–1-inch cubes

½ cup **pomegranate seeds**

a handful of **pumpkin seeds**

a good sprinkling of **gomasio** (available from health food stores)

For the dressing:

2 tablespoons **lemon juice**

½ tablespoon **tamari**

1 tablespoon **rice vinegar**

3 tablespoons **mild olive oil**

1. Bring 2 large saucepans of lightly salted water to a boil over high heat. Add the pumpkin pieces to one, reduce the heat, and simmer for about 8–10 minutes, or until just tender. Stick a knife in to test for doneness—you want them tender but not collapsing. Drain, run under cold water to stop them from cooking, then set aside to cool.

2. Add the whole purple potatoes to the other saucepan and cook for about about 15–20 minutes (depending on their size), or until just done. Drain and set aside to cool.

3. Meanwhile, heat a grill pan. Lightly oil the cobs of corn and place them on the heated grill. Keep turning them for about 10 minutes, or until they are cooked through and have some nice char markings on the sides. Remove from the pan and set aside to cool.

4. To make the dressing, mix all the ingredients together well. Taste and adjust the seasoning if you like. Aim for a salty/sour/umami flavor.

5. Now take a sharp knife and, holding the corn vertically, gently slice off the kernels.

6. Divide the salad greens evenly among 4 bowls and sprinkle with the sprouted seeds and beans.

7. Slice the cooled potatoes into disks and add them, together with the pumpkin, scallions, avocado, and corn kernels, to the bowls. Scatter each portion with the pomegranate seeds.

8. Pour the dressing over the top and scatter with the pumpkin seeds and gomasio to serve.

TIPS

*   This salad stands up well on its own, but you can also add broiled chicken or fish. If that's how you'd prefer to serve it, these quantities will serve 6.

Gill's Spinach, Chorizo & Halloumi Salad

Actually, this was created by Gill's friend Jane, but it comes to us via Gill, so we're putting her name on it. It's a salad that uses up the kinds of things you find in the refridgerator during the summer.

4 large handfuls of **baby spinach leaves,** washed
8 oz **Halloumi cheese**, cut into 4 pieces
2 fat cloves of **garlic**, crushed
¼ cup **extra virgin olive oil**, plus extra for tossing and drizzling
24 spears of **fresh asparagus**, trimmed
5 oz **chorizo**, thinly sliced
¼ cup **balsamic syrup**
salt and **freshly ground black pepper**

1. Divide the spinach among 4 large plates.

2. Lay the Halloumi cheese in a shallow dish. Mix the crushed garlic and olive oil together and pour it over the pieces of cheese and leave them to marinate for a few minutes.

3. Heat a grill pan over medium to high heat until it's very hot. Meanwhile, put the asparagus into a bowl, add a little olive oil, and toss until well coated. Season with a pinch of salt, then chargrill the asparagus spears until they are nicely lined or charred. You may want to cut a few in half lengthwise before putting them on the grill if they are really fat. Divide the asparagus among the bowls.

4. Now add the slices of Halloumi to the pan, along with the marinade. Fry the cheese until it starts to turn golden on the outside. Divide it evenly among the salad bowls, arranging it on top of the asparagus.

5. Finally, pan-fry the chorizo in a clean skillet. As it cooks, it will release plenty of its spicy oils. This is a good thing! When the sausage starts to get a little crispy on the outside, divide it up, along with the juices, on top of the 4 salads.

6. Drizzle the servings with any more olive oil that you might think is needed, and finish off with a little salt, lots of pepper, and a tablespoon of balsamic syrup per serving.

Mackerel Skies Salad

SERVES 4 AS A MAIN COURSE, OR 6 AS AN APPETIZER • PREPARATION TIME: 15 MINUTES
COOKING TIME: NONE • ♥ ✓ WF GF DF

This is FULL of omega-3 fatty acids and vitamin C, and packed with wonderful agrodolce flavor. It's quick to make, and it's colorful, too—just like a sunrise on a plate.

1 large **carrot**, grated into long strips

1 small **red bell pepper**, seeded and sliced into strips

¼ of a small **white cabbage**, shredded

1 small **raw beet**, peeled and grated

½ a large **cucumber**, peeled and cubed

7 oz **hot-smoked mackerel**, peeled and flaked

1 tablespoon **toasted flaxseeds**

For the dressing:
3 tablespoons **olive oil**
the juice of ½ a large **orange**
3 teaspoons r**ed wine vinegar**
a good pinch of **sea salt**
freshly ground black pepper

1. Put all the vegetables together in a large bowl and set aside. Add all the dressing ingredients to a clean screw-top jar. Seal securely with the lid, shake, and pour the mixture all over the vegetables. Toss together lightly to coat.

2. Stir in the flaked smoked mackerel, or scatter it on the top—it's up to you. Finish with the toasted flaxseeds.

TIPS

* Instead of mackerel, you could use hot-smoked trout or salmon. Smoked chicken works, too.

* Sometimes Kay leaves out the fish and uses the salad as a base for leftover duck or turkey.

* Mix up the seeds—we love the crunch and flavor of toasted flaxseeds, but pumpkin or sunflower would be great, too, as would walnut pieces.

A Few Words About Mackerel

Iridescent, shiny, and as fast as a bullet; as fish go, it's just about as healthy as it's possible to be. It's full of omega-3 fatty acids, vitamin B_{12}, and selenium. At the time of writing, it's one of the most sustainable fish in the sea. (Let's hope it stays that way.) And it's delicious. Smoked, broiled, steamed, or roasted—and even raw—mackerel is simply packed with flavor.

Four Simple Dressings

Tapenade Dressing

MAKES ½ CUP • PREPARATION TIME: 3 MINUTES • COOKING TIME: NONE
♥ ✓ WF DF GF (V IF YOU USE ANCHOVY-FREE TAPENADE)

Best used to dress strongly flavored salad greens or cooked greens.

> 2 tablespoons **tapenade**
> 1 tablespoon **sherry vinegar**
> ⅓ cup **extra virgin olive oil**
> **sea salt** and **freshly ground black pepper**

1. Put all the ingredients into a screw-top jar.

2. Screw on the lid, shake well, and check the seasoning.

Leon House Dressing

MAKES 2 CUPS • PREPARATION TIME: 3 MINUTES • COOKING TIME: NONE • ♥ ✓ WF DF GF V

Gives a real punch to old-fashioned lettuce leaves. Keeps well in the fridge.

> 2 tablespoons **Dijon mustard**
> ⅓ cup **white wine vinegar**
> 1½ cups **canola oil**
> **sea salt** and **freshly ground black pepper**

1. Blend the mustard and vinegar in a blender.

2. Keeping the blender running, slowly add the canola oil until you have a fully emulsified dressing.

3. Season carefully.

Balsamic Dressing

MAKES ¼ CUP • PREPARATION TIME: 3 MINUTES • COOKING TIME: NONE • ♥ ✓ WF DF GF V

Best for simple green salads with lots of chopped herbs in them.

2 tablespoons **balsamic vinegar**
(use a nice syrupy aged one if you can)
6 tablespoons **extra virgin olive oil**
(a good one really makes a difference)
sea salt and **freshly ground black pepper**

1. Put the ingredients straight onto the salad.

2. Grind lots of black pepper on top and add a generous amount of salt.

3. Toss with vigor.

Asian Dressing

MAKES ¼ CUP • PREPARATION TIME: 8 MINUTES • COOKING TIME: NONE • ♥ ✓ WF DF GF V

Best on shredded vegetables, for example, grated carrot and zucchini or finely shredded Chinese cabbage.

1 fat clove of **garlic**
½-inch piece of **fresh ginger**
1 **scallion**
½ a **fresh red chile**
1 tablespoon **Thai fish sauce**
juice of ½ a **lime**
3 tablespoons **peanut oil** or other mild oil
1 tablespoon **toasted sesame oil**

TIPS

* You can add a little
honey if you like
your dressing sweet.

1. Use your finest grater to grate the garlic and ginger into a small clean screw-top jar.

2. Finely slice the scallion, seed and finely chop the chile, and add them to the jar.

3. Measure in the fish sauce and lime juice and add the oils. Screw on the lid securely and shake well.

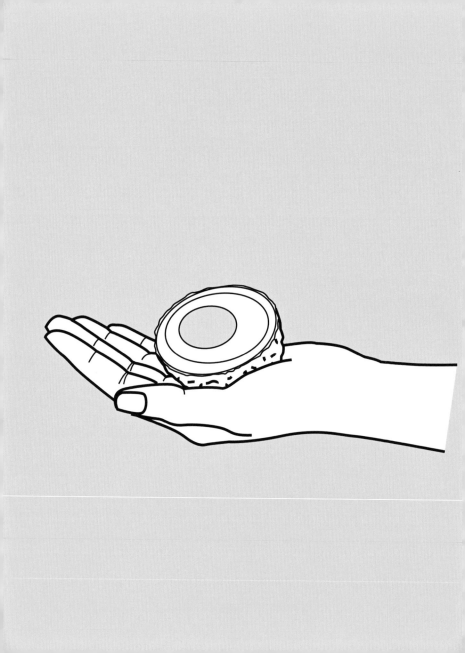

SNACKS

Benny's Scotch Eggs

SERVES 6 · PREPARATION TIME: 30 MINUTES PLUS COOLING · COOKING TIME: 20 MINUTES · ♥ ✓ WF GF

Benny Peverelli was a key part of the Leon team for eight years, a lot of that time as Executive Head Chef or Chief Foodie Personage. We love him. And we love his Scotch eggs.

7 **medium eggs**
4–5 **rice cakes**
canola oil, for deep frying (we
 reckon you'll need about 4 cups)

1 scant cup **rice flour**
2 tablespoons **milk**
6 **wheat-free, gluten-free pork
 sausages**

1. Remove the eggs from the refridgerator before you are ready to cook. When they are at room temperature, bring a medium saucepan of water to a boil. Gently lower 6 of the eggs into the boiling water and cook them for 6 minutes for soft centers, or 9 minutes for hard yolks.

2. Once the eggs are cooked, run them under cold water for 10 minutes to cool them down.

3. Gently tap the eggs all over to crack the shell, then peel them carefully because they will be soft. (Every time you take a piece of shell off, dip your fingers back into the water, otherwise they may become tacky and you could break the egg.)

4. To make the crumb mixture, break the rice cakes into small pieces, then put them into a food processor and process for a minute or so.

5. Heat the canola oil to 350°F in a deep-fat fryer. (You can do this in a heavy saucepan over medium heat, but be very VERY careful. You do so at your own risk.)

6. While the oil is heating up, prepare your crumbing station. Take 3 bowls and place the flour in one and the crumbed rice cakes in another. Break the final egg into the third bowl and whisk in the milk.

7. Cut out 2 large squares of plastic wrap. Place one on your work surface and set the other aside for later.

8. Now take a sharp knife and run it down the length of one of the sausages. Squeeze the contents of the sausage into your hand and squash together to form a ball. Repeat with the remaining sausages.

Then place each sausage ball on the plastic wrap, spaced well apart. Spread the other piece of plastic wrap out on the top and squash it down until you have 6 flat sausage ovals, about ¼ inch thick.

9. Next dry your boiled eggs with some paper towels and place one into the flour, coating it all over (this will help the sausagemeat stick). Peel a sausagemeat oval off of the plastic wrap and set the egg into it. Gently fold the sausagemeat around the egg and press the join together. Put to one side. Repeat with the other eggs.

10. Now take a small bowl of water and dampen your hands. Use your damp hands to smooth the sausage-coated eggs and turn them into smooth egg shapes.

11. Take an egg shape and gently roll it in the flour until it is well coated. Then place it in the egg and milk mixture and coat completely. Now roll it in the crumbed rice cakes to cover all over, patting the egg to make sure it all sticks. Repeat this for each egg.

12. Check that your oil is hot enough by dropping a small piece of bread into it. If the oil gently bubbles and fries the bread, it's the right temperature. Using a slotted spoon, gently lower your egg into the oil. If it's not fully submerged, carefully spoon some oil over the exposed parts of the egg. Fry for 10 minutes (or 5 on each side if your egg is not fully covered), cooking up to 3 eggs at a time.

13. Once cooked, set them on paper towels to drain. Cool for 10 minutes, then serve with ketchup or another condiment of your choice.

Ana's Cheese Empanadas

MAKES 20 SMALL EMPANADAS • PREPARATION TIME: 30 MINUTES + 30 MINUTES RESTING TIME •
COOKING TIME: 10–15 MINUTES • V

Our Ecuadorian cleaner Ana doesn't speak much English, but makes herself
understood through the language of laughter, kindness, and exceptionally good
empanadas. Great party food.

3¼ cups **all-purpose flour**
2 teaspoons **baking powder**
1 teaspoon **salt**
1 stick **butter**
¼ cup **orange juice**
⅓ cup **sparkling water**
8 oz **mozzarella cheese**
1 **onion** grated or minced
1½–2 tablespoons **superfine sugar**,
  plus extra for sprinkling on top
  (optional)
1 **egg**, lightly beaten
vegetable oil, for frying (optional)

1. Put the flour, baking powder, and salt into a food processor and
    process until well mixed.

2. Add the butter, orange juice, and sparkling water and process until a
    dough forms.

3. Tip the dough onto a work surface, bring it together into a ball, seal
    it in plastic wrap, and place in the refridgerator for 30 minutes to rest.

4. Grate the mozzarella into a bowl and add the onion. Add the sugar,
    mix well, and set aside.

5. Preheat the oven to 400°F. Line a baking sheet with parchment paper,
    or oil it well.

6. When the dough has rested remove it from the plastic wrap and dust
    your work surface with flour. Cut the ball of dough in half (it's easier
    to roll out smaller amounts). Roll out the dough so that it's as close to
    paper thin as you can make it.

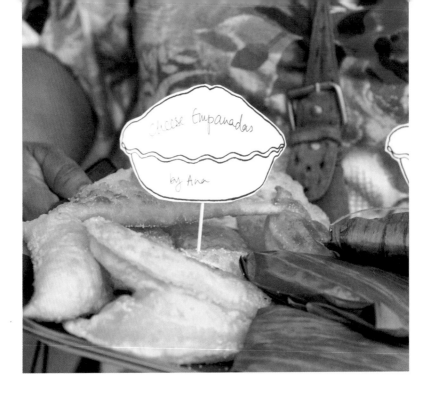

7. Using a 3½–4-inch round cookie cutter, cut out circles of dough. Place a teaspoon of the cheese filling in the center of each circle, fold the dough over to make a half-moon shape, and press down the edge with the tines of a fork. Make sure the edge is completely sealed, otherwise the filling will ooze out when you cook the empanada.

8. Brush the empanadas with the beaten egg, and sprinkle a little sugar onto each if you want that extra sweetness. Arrange them on the baking sheet and place in the oven. Bake for 10–15 minutes, or until golden. Cool on a wire rack.

9. If you prefer the fried option, place a saucepan over medium heat and fill with vegetable oil to a depth of 2 inches. When the oil is hot, deep-fry the empanadas until golden. Sprinkle with sugar to serve.

Things on Potatoes

SERVES 4 • PREPARATION TIME: 5 MINUTES • COOKING TIME: I HOUR • ♥ ✓ WF GF DF V

Sometimes there's nothing better than a hot baked potato, crusty on the outside and steaming and soft within, just begging to be buttered. But what else can we do with them? Here are some suggestions from family and friends for making the best baked potatoes ever…

1. Pick your potato. This is very important. Buy a variety that bakes well—high-starch types are best. We recommend russets.

2. Heat the oven to 425°F.

3. Wash the potatoes under cold running water. Shake them a little to remove the excess water, but don't dry them completely.

4. Roll them in some sea salt.

5. Put them straight into the oven, directly onto the rack. Bake them for about an hour—it depends on the size of your potato. Just poke them with a skewer to test for "give" and doneness.

6. Take them out and let everyone admire their crispy exterior and be amazed at their fluffy insides.

Some ideas for toppings, from left to right:

Georgia's Eggy Potato

Scoop out the insides of the cooked potato. Mash it in a bowl with a lightly beaten egg, then season. Add some crisply fried bacon bits (or leftover ham), and some cheese, if you desire, or any pieces of cooked vegetables you have on hand. Scoop it all back into the potato skin, put a pat of butter on top, and return to the oven for 15 minutes, or until it's puffy and crispy on top.

Cheesy Spinach & Mushrooms

This is for Abi and Issy, the vegetarian element of our team. Sauté some sliced mushrooms in a little olive oil and butter with a scattering of garlic and parsley, and set aside. Then wilt down a handful or two of spinach in the same saucepan. Season with salt and pepper. Pile it onto the potato with the mushrooms and add some cubed Gruyère cheese on top.

Eleanor's Make the Grade Potatoes

Eleanor is John's younger daughter. One day at school in first grade she was allowed to sit with Mr. and Mrs. Heinrich, and to have baked potatoes with her favorite topping: plenty of butter and EXTRA shredded Cheddar cheese, salt, and black pepper. Now that's what we call making the grade.

Beet, Crème Fraiche & Chives

Simply chop some cooked (not pickled) beets into cubes. Spoon some crème fraîche onto the buttered potato. Scatter with the beet cubes and finish with chopped fresh chives, salt, and black pepper.

Herb Butter

Very retro, but very good. Make the herb butter of your choice—we use finely chopped fresh parsley, garlic, fresh thyme, and salt and black pepper mashed into some softened unsalted butter. If you have time, using some plastic wrap or foil, roll the soft butter into a sausage shape and refrigerate it. Then just slice off a few disks and place them artfully in a steaming, split potato.

The Leftover Potato

Baked potatoes take to leftovers like ducks to water (actually, leftover duck would be fantastic). So, use 'em up.

THE LEFTOVER POTATO

Arthur's Favorite Duck & Lettuce Wraps

SERVES 4 CHILDREN • PREPARATION TIME: 5 MINUTES • COOKING TIME: 25 MINUTES • WF GF DF

A healthy and fun dish for the children to help make.

> 1 **cucumber**
> 2 **Boston lettuce**
> 1 **duck breast**
> **olive oil**
> **plum sauce**, to serve
> **sea salt** and **freshly ground black pepper**

1. Preheat the oven to 375°F. Cut the cucumber into batons and put into a bowl. Separate the lettuce leaves, wash and spin them dry, and put them into a second bowl.

2. Season the duck breast and add a dash of olive oil and roast for about 25 minutes, or until the skin is crispy. Shred the cooked meat into little pieces, using 2 forks.

3. Get the children to make parcels, wrapping the duck and cucumber in the lettuce leaves, and serve the plum sauce separately on the side in a small bowl.

Fish Stick Wrap

SERVES 2 · PREPARATION TIME: 10 MINUTES · COOKING TIME: 20 MINUTES · ♥ ✓

Every kid's favorite… in a wrap.

4 **fish sticks**
2 good-quality **flatbreads**
2 tablespoons good **tartar sauce**
4–6 **pickles**, sliced
Romaine lettuce leaves, shredded

a pinch of chopped **fresh dill**
a squeeze of **lemon juice**
salt and **freshly ground black pepper**

1. Cook the fish sticks and heat up your flatbreads according to the package instructions.

2. Spread some tartar sauce onto the warmed flatbreads, and add a few pickle slices. Add some lettuce, then the crisply cooked fish sticks. Scatter with freshly chopped dill, season with salt and pepper, and get fancy with a squeeze of fresh lemon juice to finish. Wrap and eat.

Leon's Halloumi Wrap

SERVES 2 · PREPARATION TIME: 10 MINUTES · COOKING TIME: 6 MINUTES · ♥ ✓ V

This is based on the popular wrap we had on the menu for a while. Time to bring it back?

2 tablespoons good **mango chutney**
2 gluten-free **flatbreads**, or the **flatbread** of your choice
7 oz **halloumi cheese**, sliced and marinated in **olive oil**, crushed **garlic**, and **thyme leaves**

2 **carrots**, peeled and grated
2 tablespoons **fresh flat-leaf parsley**, chopped
salt and **freshly ground black pepper**

1. Spread the mango chutney thinly on the flatbread of your choice.

2. Drain the cheese and grill it for 3 minutes or so on each side, until golden brown.

3. Put half of the halloumi into each flatbread (heat them up if you like) and add the carrot, parsley and freshly ground black pepper. Add some salt if you really want it. Wrap and eat.

Things on Toast

SERVES 4 · PREPARATION TIME: 15 MINUTES · COOKING TIME: 10 MINUTES · ♥ ✓ WF GF DF V

Toast, glorious toast. Sometimes we just need to jazz it up a little. Here are some suggestions from the Leon team:

Brown Crabmeat, Lemon & Dill

Spread some thick brown crabmeat on your toast. Squeeze some lemon juice onto it. Finish with freshly ground black pepper and scatter with chopped fresh dill.

Marmite, Avocado, Tomato, Basil & Gomasio

Kay's favorite: spread a smear of good unsalted butter on the toast. Then a smear of Marmite. Follow this with sliced avocados and halved cherry tomatoes. Add a couple fresh basil leaves, a good grinding of black pepper. Scatter with Gomasio.

Graig Farm's All-Meat Sausage on Fig Preserves

Broil or oven-roast some sausages until cooked. Spread the toast with a thick layer of fig preserves. Slice the sausages in half lengthwise and arrange them on the toast.

Poached Egg & Sautéed Mushrooms

Slice some mushrooms and sauté them with some garlic in a little olive oil. Scatter with a few leaves of fresh thyme or some chopped fresh parsley. Set aside but keep warm while you poach an egg. Pile the mushrooms on the toast and set the poached egg on top.

Goat Cheese, Honey, Thyme & Walnuts

Preheat the broiler on high. Cut a goat cheese log (the type with a rind) into slices. Place 2 or 3 slices overlapping on each slice of toast. Place under the broiler for 1 minute, or just until the cheese is melting slightly. Drizzle with honey and scatter with chopped walnuts and fresh thyme.

Cinnamon Butter with Sliced Apples

Mix some softened butter with a good pinch of ground cinnamon and a spoonful of agave syrup to taste. Spread on the toast. Arrange slices of raw apple on top and dust with a little more ground cinnamon.

Dips

Hummus

SERVES 4–6 • PREPARATION TIME: 10 MINUTES • COOKING TIME: NONE • ♥ ✓ WF GF V

Everybody loves hummus. Our supermarkets sell it by the ton—literally. But have you seen what's written on the label? Try this homemade version, and cut out the additives.

1 x 15-oz can of **chickpeas**, drained
1–2 cloves of **garlic**, peeled
2 tablespoons **tahini**
2 tablespoons **olive oil**
6 tablespoons **water**
the juice of ½ a **lemon**

a large pinch of **salt**
extra virgin olive oil, for drizzling
ground sumac and/or **ground cumin**, for sprinkling (optional)

1. Place everything except the oil and the sumac/cumin in a food processor and process until smooth. Taste and adjust the seasoning.

2. Serve in a bowl, drizzled with a little extra virgin olive oil. Sprinkle with the sumac and/or cumin before serving, if you like.

Lentil Masala Dip

SERVES 4–6 • PREPARATION TIME: 5 MINUTES + COOLING • COOKING TIME: 10–20 MINUTES • ♥ ✓ WF GF V

Fragrant with curry and highly addictive.

¾ cup **red lentils**
1 teaspoon **Madras curry powder**
a pinch of **ground ginger**

a small handful of **fresh cilantro**, chopped
salt and **freshly ground black pepper**

1. Rinse the lentils well under running water to get rid of any grit or sand. Add them to a saucepan over high heat and cover with fresh cold water.

2. Bring to a boil and simmer for about 15 minutes, or following the package instructions. Drain and set aside to cool.

3. Once the lentils have cooled, process them in a food processor with the curry powder, ground ginger, salt, and pepper. Taste and adjust the seasoning, then stir in the chopped cilantro and serve.

Tangy Cheese Dip

SERVES 4 · PREPARATION TIME: 10 MINUTES · COOKING TIME: NONE · ♥ ✓ WF GF V

Cottage cheese isn't just for dieter's fruit plates.

1¾ cups **cottage cheese**
1 clove of **garlic**, peeled and chopped
1 tablespoon **Worcestershire sauce**
1 teaspoon **tomato ketchup**
½ teaspoon **Tabasco sauce**
a good squeeze of **lime** or **lemon juice**
1 tablespoon chopped **fresh chives**
4 **cherry tomatoes**, seeded and chopped
a small handful of **fresh cilantro**, chopped
1 large **red chile**, seeded and slivered (optional)
salt and **freshly ground black pepper**

1. Process everything except the chives, tomatoes, cilantro, and chile in a food processor. Taste and adjust the seasoning. Aim for a little spice, some sharpness, and some sweetness.

2. Pour into a serving bowl and gently stir in the chives and tomatoes. Scatter with chopped cilantro and the slivered chiles, if using.

Kay's Guacamole

SERVES 4 · PREPARATION TIME: 10 MINUTES · COOKING TIME: NONE · ♥ ✓ WF GF DF V

Rich, green, and good for you.

1 clove of **garlic**, peeled
2 ripe **avocados**, peeled and the flesh scooped out
the juice of ½ a **lime**
2 **scallions**, trimmed and finely chopped
a small handful of **fresh cilantro**, finely chopped
½–1 **green serrano** or **jalapeño chile**, seeded and minced (optional)
4 **cherry tomatoes**, sliced (optional)
sea salt, to taste

1. Using a big mortar and pestle or a molcajete, grind the garlic to a paste. Add the avocado and pound until mashed. Add the lime juice.

2. Stir in the chopped scallions and the chopped cilantro. If using, stir in the chiles and the tomatoes. Season to taste with salt.

Roasted Carrot & Cumin Dip

SERVES 4–6 • PREPARATION TIME: 10 MINUTES • COOKING TIME: 50 MINUTES • ♥ WF GF DF V

Healthy and simple. And bright orange.

10–12 **carrots** (about 1½ lbs), coarsely chopped
3 tablespoons **olive oil**
a pinch of **sugar** (optional)
1 teaspoon **ground cumin**
1 clove of **garlic**, peeled and coarsely crushed
2 tablespoons **water**
salt and **freshly ground black pepper**

1. Heat the oven to 400°F.

2. Toss the carrots in a roasting pan with 1 tablespoon of the olive oil, a pinch of sugar (if you feel like it), and a good sprinkle of salt and pepper.

3. Cover with aluminum foil and roast for 45–50 minutes, or until a knife goes through the carrots easily.

4. Remove from the oven and let cool slightly.

5. Once the carrots have cooled, put them into the food processor or blender and process, adding the cumin, garlic, and the remaining 2 tablespoons of olive oil and the water, until you have a nice creamy consistency. Serve at room temperature.

CONVERSION CHART FOR COMMON MEASURES

LIQUIDS

15 ml	$\frac{1}{2}$ fl oz
25 ml	1 fl oz
50 ml	2 fl oz
75 ml	3 fl oz
100ml	3 $\frac{1}{2}$ fl oz
125 ml	4 fl oz
150 ml	$\frac{1}{4}$ pint
175 ml	6 fl oz
200 ml	7 fl oz
250 ml	8 fl oz
275 ml	9 fl oz
300 ml	$\frac{1}{2}$ pint
325 ml	11 fl oz
350 ml	12 fl oz
375 ml	13 fl oz
400 ml	14 fl oz
450 ml	$\frac{3}{4}$ pint
475 ml	16 fl oz
500 ml	17 fl oz
575 ml	18 fl oz
600 ml	1 pint
750 ml	1 $\frac{1}{4}$ pints
900 ml	1 $\frac{1}{2}$ pints
1 liter	1 $\frac{3}{4}$ pints
1.2 liters	2 pints
1.5 liters	2 $\frac{1}{2}$ pints
1.8 liters	3 pints
2 liters	3 $\frac{1}{2}$ pints
2.5 liters	4 pints
3.6 liters	6 pints

WEIGHTS

5 g	$\frac{1}{4}$ oz
15 g	$\frac{1}{2}$ oz
20 g	$\frac{3}{4}$ oz
25 g	1 oz
50 g	2 oz
75 g	3 oz
125 g	4 oz
150 g	5 oz
175 g	6 oz
200 g	7 oz
250 g	8 oz
275 g	9 oz
300 g	10 oz
325 g	11 oz
375 g	12 oz
400 g	13 oz
425 g	14 oz
475 g	15 oz
500 g	1 lb
625 g	1 $\frac{1}{4}$ lb
750 g	1 $\frac{1}{2}$ lb
875 g	1 $\frac{3}{4}$ lb
1 kg	2 lb
1.25 kg	2 $\frac{1}{2}$ lb
1.5 kg	3 lb
1.75 kg	3 $\frac{1}{2}$ lb
2 kg	4 lb

OVEN TEMPERATURES

225°F ......(110°C) ......Gas Mark $1/4$

250°F ......(120°C) ......Gas Mark $1/2$

275°F ......(140°C) ......Gas Mark 1

300°F ......(150°C) ......Gas Mark 2

325°F ......(160°C) ......Gas Mark 3

350°F ......(180°C) ......Gas Mark 4

375°F ......(190°C) ......Gas Mark 5

400°F ......(200°C) ......Gas Mark 6

425°F ......(220°C) ......Gas Mark 7

450°F ......(230°C) ......Gas Mark 8

Working with different types of oven

All the recipes in this book have been tested in an oven without a fan. If you are using a convection (fan-assisted) oven, lower the temperature setting by 25°F. Convection ovens circulate heat evenly and efficiently around the oven, so there's no need to worry about where to position the baking dish.

Regardless of what type of oven you use you will find each has its idiosyncrasies, so don't stick slavishly to any baking recipe instructions. Make sure you understand how your oven behaves and adjust to that.

Key to Symbols/Nutritional Info

♥	LOW SATURATED FATS
✓	LOW GLYCEMIC (GI) LOAD
WF	WHEAT FREE
GF	GLUTEN FREE
DF	DAIRY FREE
V	VEGETARIAN
🍴	INDULGENCE
🐦 TIPS	COOKING TIPS, EXTRA INFORMATION, AND ALTERNATIVE IDEAS.

MEASUREMENTS

5 mm	....	$1/4$ inch
1 cm	....	$1/2$ inch
1.5 cm	....	$3/4$ inch
2.5 cm	....	1 inch
5 cm	....	2 inches
7 cm	....	3 inches
10 cm	....	4 inches
12 cm	....	5 inches
15 cm	....	6 inches
18 cm	....	7 inches
20 cm	....	8 inches
23 cm	....	9 inches
25 cm	....	10 inches
28 cm	....	11 inches
30 cm	....	12 inches
33 cm	....	13 inches

Index

First published in Great Britain in 2013
by Conran Octopus Limited,
a part of Octopus Publishing Group,
Endeavour House, 189 Shaftesbury Avenue,
London WC2H 8JY
www.octopusbooks.co.uk

Reprinted in 2013

An Hachette UK Company
www.hachette.co.uk

Distributed in the US by Hachette Book Group USA
237 Park Avenue, New York NY 10017 USA

Distributed in Canada by Canadian Manda Group
165 Dufferin Street, Toronto, Ontario, Canada
M6K 3H6

This book includes a selection of previously
published recipes taken from the following titles:
Leon Naturally Fast Food; *Leon Baking & Puddings*;
Leon Family & Friends.

Publisher: Alison Starling
Senior Editor: Sybella Stephens
Assistant Editor: Stephanie Milner
Art Director: Jonathan Christie
Art Direction, Design and Illustrations:
   Anita Mangan
Design Assistant: Abigail Read
Photography: Georgia Glynn Smith
Production Manager: Katherine Hockley

ISBN 978 1 84091 632 4

Printed in China

A note from the authors…
Medium eggs should be used unless otherwise
stated. We have endeavored to be as accurate as
possible in all the preparation and cooking times
listing in the recipes in this book. However they are
an estimate based on our own timings during
recipe testing, and should be taken as a guide only,
not as the literal truth. We have also tried to source
all our food facts carefully. However, we are not
scientists,
so our food facts and nutrition advice are not
absolute. If you feel you require consultation with
a nutritionist, consult your famwily doctor or
healthcare provider for a recommendation.